# WHEN D. CALLED BEATRICE
## (2nd edition)

by

## Rodney Wood

The Woodener Press

ISBN: 9798840399842
2nd Edition Published by The Woodener Press
Copyright © Rodney Wood 2022
All rights reserved
Email: rodneytwood@gmail.com
Website: https: rodneywoodpoet.wordpress.com

9 Monks Close
Farnborough
Hants
GU14 7DB

The right of Rodney Wood to be identified as the author of this work has been asserted in accordance with Section 77 of the Copyright, Design and Patents Act 1988.

Please direct all enquiries to the author

Acknowledgements: I would like to thank the editors of the following magazines who published these poems, or versions of them: Ditch ('Come Dancing'), Hinterland ('Actually, I Did'), The Journal ('After Goethe', 'The Pedestrian Night'), The Lake ('The Aegean Tercet', 'My Selfishness'), Message In A Bottle ('How Far We must Go', 'The Sheet Of Night'), Stride ('Quick'), The Weary Blues ('Loving Notary of Your Intimacies'), Screech Owl ('About You, If Anyone's Asking', 'Baby Here I Come').

Thanks also to Mark Cobley of The Red Ceiling Press for publishing the first edition of this book in 2017 and giving permission to publish this second edition includes additional poems.

Printed and bound in the UK

# Contents

Frances. Frances.
Frances. Frances.

# DANTE CALLED YOU BEATRICE

of the dark blossom in your eyes
                                  of the electric cello of your body
lines speaking of desire
                        of the dark blossom in your eyes
lines speaking of desire
                       of the electric cello of your body


with many a clumsy phrase
                   I've written so many lyrics
                                    that fall flat
calling attention to my lunacy
                        with many a clumsy phrase
calling attention to my lunacy
                   I've written so many lyrics
                                    that fall flat


to using those three simple words
                   & just said
                        *I love you*
I should have gone back
                   to using those three simple words
I should have gone back
                   & just said
                        *I love you*

# LOVER ON DOVER BEACH

& it's you I want to hold
                    I want the touch
                                of your hands
wherever I turn
            I see you clearly
                        & it's you I want to hold
wherever I turn
            I see you clearly
                        I want the touch
                                    of your hands


a blessing of angels singing
                            or the world
                                    breaking out in peace
it's like a miracle
                a flash of lightning
                            a blessing of angels singing
it's like a miracle
                a flash of lightning
                            or the world
                                    breaking out in peace


everywhere I turn you're there
                        & you've taken my macho
                                        my ego
I've forgotten how I should live
                        everywhere I turn you're there
I've forgotten how I should live
                        & you've taken my macho
                                        my ego

# STANDING STILL STANDING

& I'm the sea
   drawing on the beach
     & I'm gently licking your quartz
sometimes you're a stretch of sand
    & I'm the sea
      drawing on the beach
sometimes you're a stretch of sand
     & I'm gently licking your quartz


the afternoons
   the notebooks full of poems
     the grey skies
      the waiting
I forget cold morning
   the afternoons
    the notebooks full of poems
I forget cold morning
   the grey skies
     the waiting


like a voice
  a river
   a faint breeze
    your smile dazzling light & fire
& suddenly you're there
   like a voice
     a river
      a faint breeze
& suddenly you're there
   your smile dazzling light & fire

# WE ONLY DIE WHEN LOVE PERISHES

winceyette pyjamas
        because nights were arctic
                & that put an end to lust
it wasn't our dream
        winceyette pyjamas
it wasn't our dream
        because nights were arctic
                & that put an end to lust


with its requests for payment
        children
            work etc.
              & life became ordinary
the mesozoic period
        with its requests for payment
                children
the mesozoic period
        work etc.
          & life became ordinary


152"
      HD
          plasma display
              that ultimate
                all round experience
our love is desire & grace
          152"
            HD
            plasma display

our love is desire & grace
        that ultimate
            all round experience

# A SEED OF LIGHT IN MY HANDS

*"who could release a woman*
        *or dream there was a key"* Tom Pickard 'Window'


because all I think about is you
                        as soon as my pen touches the paper
I sit
            & can't think what to write
                                because all I think about is you
I sit
            & can't think what to write
                        as soon as my pen touches the paper


the sun & the moon
                that sing only for you
                        the trees that shelter you from rain
the smell of apples you carry round
                            the sun & the moon
                                    that sing only for you
the smell of apples you carry round
                        the trees that shelter you from rain


the pink tongue
                the alphabet of you
                        your voice smouldering in my ears
the long notes drawn against the sky
                        the pink tongue
                                the alphabet of you
the long notes drawn against the sky
                        your voice smouldering in my ears

# QUICK

before water changes
         into beer & whisky
                before my flaccid penis
                becomes obvious
before the bomb disposal van arrives
                before water changes
                into beer & whisky
before the bomb disposal van arrives
                before my flaccid penis
                becomes obvious


before the scream & veins of death
                before someone
                      plays the piano
before I'm taken into custody
           or worse
                before the scream & veins of
death
before I'm taken into custody
           or worse
                before someone
                      plays the piano


before someone tells me
           *get up*
                before I leap towards
                      the impossible
& there is nothing else to say
                before someone tells me
                      *get up*
& there is nothing else to say
                before I leap towards
                      the impossible

# LONG AFTER (RILKE)

branches of ash naked
                against the soft light
                                a smear of winter light
                                        the flag of sky
cars like candles on the river
                            branches of ash naked
                                    against the soft light
cars like candles on the river
                          a smear of winter light
                                        the flag of sky


it follows you round like a song
                            it becomes confused with the moon
there's one star in the sky
                        a burning mass
                                  it follows you round like a bird
there's one star in the sky
                        a burning mass
                      it becomes confused with the moon


they reach back to nothing
                                & everything was all so amazing
the galaxies send radio signals
                        wave emissions
                              they reach back to nothing
the galaxies send radio signals
                        wave emissions
                              & everything was all so amazing

# KEEP FAITH

but all I do
      is make them empty
            as if my senses were a wasteland
I mess with words
      but all I do
            is make them empty
I mess with words
      as if my senses were a wasteland


my hands believe a touch
      means death
         & my eyes are blind
            with desire
I can't capture your gestures
      my hands believe a touch
         means death
I can't capture your gestures
      & my eyes are blind
         with desire


& I would not leave the world
      even though it's full of deceit
         indifferent & aloof
I have this constant need for you
      & I would not leave the world
I have this constant need for you
      even though it's full of deceit
         indifferent & aloof

# THE AEGEAN TERCET

cafés spill wine
    & coffee onto streets
        & women with pots
         & wicker baskets
I sit on a bench
    & see cafés spill wine
        & coffee onto streets
I sit on a bench & see
    & women with pots
        & wicker baskets


drunks bellow from a pirate ship
    & their laughter splits the air
        soars & bites
they think life is fun
    the drunks
    from a pirate ship
they think life is fun
    the drunks
    & their laughter splits the air
        soars & bites


at the hotel
    you glance at the room
        your eyes a beacon
         for me
          who's lost
after an hour or so I go back
    at the hotel
        you glance at the room
after an hour or so I go back
    your eyes a beacon
        for me
         who's lost

# AFTER GOETHE

every word I say is a kiss
                    & I want to keep talking with you
your breath & desire fill my body
                    every word I say is a kiss
your breath & desire fill my body
                    & I want to keep talking with you


the loved voice of the present
                    I watch your eyes
                              light & shadow
stabbed by a ray of sun
                    the loved voice of the present
stabbed by a ray of sun
                    I watch your eyes
                              light & shadow


an earthquake or fire-storm
                    & I think is it the end
                              or another weekend
the old masters
          shock & desolation
                    an earthquake or fire-storm
the old masters
          shock & desolation
                    & I think is it the end
                              or another weekend

# LOVE WITH A GLASS OF RIOJA

I lay alone with days
           with my tears
                   & glass of rioja
I'm at the beach
           I lay alone with days
I'm at the beach
         with my tears
              & glass of rioja


I dive deep inside your eyes
               where love
                   is a burning stream
your voice comes from the sea
            I dive deep inside your eyes
your voice comes from the sea
               where love
                   is a burning stream


I'm scared I'll never see you again
           & I'll not hear your voice
tears
       the colour of eyes
              I'm scared I'll never see you again
tears
       the colour of eyes
          & I'll not hear your voice

# SHARING TONGUES

I want to share tongues with you
        I want to tell you how much I love you
I want to talk with my lips
        I want to share tongues with you
I want to talk with my lips
        I want to tell you how much I love you


as my mind overflows with rubbish
        & my voice refuses to obey me
every day I fail to say
    *I love you*
        as my mind overflows with rubbish
every day I fail to say
    *I love you*
        & my voice refuses to obey me


& I talk about a thousand things
        & I've never felt like this
I'm stupid
    petty & unnecessary
        & I talk about a thousand things
I'm stupid
    petty & unnecessary
        & I've never felt like this

# A SUMMER AFTERNOON LIKE THIS

a terrible love chokes me
                    & I've never felt like this
I open my eyes
              I repeat myself
                              a terrible love chokes me
I open my eyes
              I repeat myself
                              & I've never felt like this


I run out to the empty street
                          & it dazzles me
                                      this harmless lunatic
I stumble again in shadows
                      I run out to the empty street
                                          & it dazzles me
I stumble again in shadows
                          this harmless lunatic


I want to tell of words
              that are feral & sweet
                              words that sway
                                      & sigh in my head
something is devouring me
                      I want to tell of woes
                                  that are feral & sweet
something is devouring me
                      words that sway
                              & sigh in my head

# BEGINNING WITH A PHRASE BY UMBERTO SABA

it's snowing
                      each flake is a word
                                      I love you for listening to me
it's taken 30 years to write this
                                    it's snowing
                                            each flake is a word
it's taken 30 years to write this
                                    I love you for listening to me


the afternoons
                      the notebooks full of poems
                                    the helplessness
                                        the waiting
sometimes I forget the cold mornings
                                  the afternoons
                                      the notebooks full of poems
sometimes I forget the cold mornings
                                  the helplessness
                                      the waiting


like a white tree
                      full of memories
                                  our smiles
                                          melt the snow
& suddenly you're there
                                  like a white tree
                                    full of memories
& suddenly you're there
                                our smiles
                                melt the snow

# THE PEDESTRIAN NIGHT

drunk with wine & love & song
                    it can't believe it's lying next to you
pity my poor winceyette soul
                        drunk with wine & love & song
pity my poor winceyette soul
                    it can't believe it's lying next to you


between duvet & 100% cotton sheet
                    across the linen to the memory of you
my hands are wanton
                they fumble
                    between duvet & 100% cotton sheet
my hands are wanton
                they fumble
                    across the linen to the memory of you


in the deep
        the warm silence of sleep
                        but the bed wants to hear
                                our moans
you stay immersed in dreams
                    in the deep
                        the warm silence of sleep
you stay immersed in dreams
                    but the bed wants to hear
                                our moans

# DISTANCE

the tall ships of sleep sailing over night
                              kiss me
                                    & bring the soft light of dawn
my heart is a river
                    the prow of a ship
                              the tall ships of sleep sailing over night
my heart is a river
                    the prow of a ship
                              kiss me
                                    & bring the soft light of dawn


the glow of light
                    the recollection of a song
                              & the tenderness of sleeping hours
the bare recollection of dreams
                              the glow of light
                                    the recollection of a song
the bare recollection of dreams
                              & the tenderness of sleeping hours


the hours long before waking
                              the surreal trance
                                    & meandering words
but somehow I have to live through
                              the long hours before waking
but somehow I have to live through
                              the surreal trance
                                    & meandering words

# VOICES & BOURBON

knowing I have you to love
                            life has stopped leaking away
euphoria
                an immense light
                                    knowing I have you to love
euphoria
                an immense light
                                    life has stopped leaking away


from a wedding & someone's party
                            along with too much cheap booze
I'm dazed
            with a hangover caught
                            from a wedding & someone's party
I'm dazed
            with a hangover caught
                                    along with too much cheap
booze


I dream of smoke
                        roses & you
                        & night is ringing in my mouth
I'm wearing my favourite shoes
                            I dream of smoke
                                        roses & you
I'm wearing my favourite shoes
                        & night is ringing in my mouth

# LINES THAT NEED NO TITLE

lose my self in the folds of your clothes
                                & enjoy the shelter of your kisses
sometimes I want to hold you
                                lose my self in the folds of your clothes
sometimes I want to hold you
                                & enjoy the shelter of your kisses


where we used to go for a walk
                                & the flowers we grew in an old box
sometimes I remember the garden
                                   where we used to go for a walk
sometimes I remember the garden
                                & the flowers we grew in an old box


& said out loud how much I love you
                                me who could almost be called a youth
sometimes I thought you were a goddess
                                & said out loud how much I love you
sometimes I thought you were a goddess
                                me who could almost be called a youth

# MY SELFISHNESS

over a sea of whiteness
                    a solitary hand moves
                                        with tranquillity
I write these poems each evening
                                over a sea of whiteness
I write these poems each evening
                            a solitary hand moves
                                        with tranquillity


& you're close to my lips
                    as delicate & smooth
                                        as an angel
streetlamps flicker over ash & oak
                            & you're close to my lips
streetlamps flicker over ash & oak
                        as delicate & smooth
                                    as an angel


with paper pen & ink
                        I can never be alone while writing
if I had to choose
            I'd stay here
                            with paper pen & ink
if I had to choose
            I'd stay here
                        I can never be alone while writing

# INSTEAD OF A SONNET

the poetry & pleasure
                    of your moans
                            the lips that desire only me
I long for you
            your voice
                    the poetry & pleasure
                                    of your moans
I long for you
            your voice
                    the lips that desire only me


my love flies out to you singing
                            its voice can only praise you
when my heart opens
                    my love flies out to you singing
when my heart opens
                    its voice can only praise you


all the world will be rearranged
                            & your sun will flood my eyes
I expect wonders around every corner
                            all the world will be rearranged
I expect wonders around every corner
                            & your sun will flood my eyes

# ACTUALLY I DID

returned with incredible footage of me
                                 & you under a lime tree bower
spent the day at Coleridge cottage
                        returned with incredible footage of me
spent the day at Coleridge cottage
                                 & you under a lime tree bower


my ring
        a pull tab
                your ring
                        6 florescent diamonds
blessed in the Elvis chapel
                my ring
                        a pull tab
blessed in the Elvis chapel
                your ring
                      6 florescent diamonds


I hired a photographer for this
                          I don't want people thinking I made it up
the reception was at McDonald's
                          I hired a photographer for this
the reception was at McDonald's
                          I don't want people thinking I made it up

# LOVING NOTARY OF YOUR INTIMACIES

round as the ring of grace
                        that surround you love
when all the birds have fled
                        round as the ring of grace
when all the birds have fled
                        that surround you love


like a prize at a fairground
                        a vase
                                a watch
                                        a box of chocolates
the moon's a gift tied with ribbon
                                like a prize at a fairground
the moon's a gift tied with ribbon
                        a vase
                                a watch
                                        a box of chocolates


an impressionist garden
                        filled with a divine light
moments with you are wine
                                an impressionist garden
moments with you are wine
                        filled with a divine light

# THINKING OF BECOMING MYSELF

scrawl meaningless phrases
                  images
                       sound
                             heat & sense
I write like shit
          scrawl meaningless phrases
I write like shit
       images
              sounds
                    heat & sense


an alphabet that leaks from my pen
                         I want to share something
I write like shit
          an alphabet that leaks from my pen
I write like shit
          I want to share something


I dream of villanelles
          pantoums
                I surrender to the pleasure of words
                           & you
I write like shit but
                I dream of villanelles
                      pantoums
I write like shit but
                I surrender to the pleasure of words
                           & you

# KNOWING

you built the ship I sail

        you're my lighthouse & harbour

maybe you'll hear this

        you built ship I sail

maybe you'll hear this

        you're my lighthouse & harbour


you're the compass that guides me

        you're the sea that welcomes me

maybe you'll hear this

        you're the compass that guides me

maybe you'll hear this

        you're the sea that welcomes me


all I can say is

        *I love you*

           & love's like breathing

              it's that easy

maybe you'll hear this

        all I can say is

          *I love you*

maybe you'll hear this

        & love's like breathing

              it's that easy

# THE SIMPLE WORDS

so I must use
   the simple words
      those veined with lust & power
I cannot speak
   with flowery phrases
      so I must use
       the simple words
I cannot speak
   with flowery phrases
      those veined with lust & power


& all I can think about is you
     my dear
       even when
        you will no longer be with me
let me say
  love is everything
     & all I can think about is you
        my dear
let me say
  love is everything
     even when
      you will no longer be with me


it comes running overs horizons as light
      it comes like an animal
        cold & dark
nothing will ever erase your name
      it comes running overs horizons as light
nothing will ever erase your name
      it comes like an animal
        cold & dark

# GIVING LUST SOME DIGNITY

so much love
            dreams & wine
                        sunk to the bottom of your eyes
buried under salt
           silt & sand
               so much love
                      dreams & wine
buried under salt
           silt & sand
               sunk to the bottom of your eyes


we're reading from the same book
                    your hands are soft & tired
I'm an old boat adrift in your harbour
               we're reading from the same book
I'm an old boat adrift in your harbour
                    your hands are soft & tired


you speak of light & understanding
                    your name is free as the sea
you're modest sweet & faithful
               you speak of light & understanding
you're modest sweet & faithful
                  your name is free as the sea

# TOWARDS A MARCH SONGBOOK

& it makes me feel strange & lost
        & the world is dark & eclipsed
a grim smile unfolds on your face
       & it makes me feel strange & lost
a grim smile unfolds on your face
        & the world is dark & eclipsed


not hinting at that other sweeter side
        hidden behind the noisy moon
it's a mask you wear
       not hinting at that other sweeter side
it's a mask you wear
      hidden behind the noisy moon


I have to use a solar filter sheet
      I see only the gleam in your eyes
when I look at your face
      I have to use a solar filter sheet
when I look at your face
      I see only the gleam in your eyes

# & ALWAYS YOU'RE THERE

& there's you rising
        like treasure
               it has to climb each wave
                  before it fades
I can tell that the sea is tired & sad
             & there's you rising
                like treasure
I can tell that the sea is tired & sad
             it has to climb each wave
                before it fades

it has to climb each tree
        before it falls
          & there's you soaring
             like a mountain
I can tell that the earth is tired & sad
          it has to climb each tree
            before it falls
I can tell that the earth is tired & sad
          & there's you soaring
             like a mountain

it has to climb higher
        each night
          & there's you dragging
             the sun behind
I can tell that the sky is tired & sad
          it has to climb higher
            each night
I can tell that the sky is tired & sad
          & there's you dragging
             the sun behind

# THE DIAMOND I NEVER LOST

I want to be the clothes that caress you
           I want to touch the petal of your lips
here I am writing again
           I want to be the clothes that caress you
here I am writing again
           I want to touch the petal of your lips


the sacred rose
        & silver maiden grass you hold
           the stiff vase with clear water
I love the shelter of your eyes
        the sacred rose
        & silver maiden grass you hold
I love the shelter of your eyes
           the stiff vase with clear water


that surrounds me
        like a song & holy hours
           that watches me
             quilting with words
you're the passion of my life that
           surrounds me
           like a song & holy hours
you're the passion of my life that
           watches me
             quilting with words

# WORDS ARE WIND

through rusty locks & crannies
                              through iron gates & narrow alleys
the wind blows through our house
                              through rusty locks & crannies
the wind blows through our house
                              through iron gates & narrow alleys


I can barely see you standing
                              but I can feel you holding my hand
the wind is full of smells & memories
                              I can barely see you standing
the wind is full of smells & memories
                              but I can feel you holding my hand

it's a simples thing the wind carries
                              & people think I'm crazy
I'm stunned
        I'm drunk
              I'm amazed
                    it's a simples thing in the wind carries
I'm stunned
        I'm drunk
              I'm amazed
                    & people think I'm crazy

# A VOICE THAT WAVERS

with a voice that wavers
                              like the smoke of a censer
I speak in the twilight of words
                                   with a voice that wavers
I speak in the twilight of words
                              like the smoke of a censer


to discover the murmur of your breath
                              because you're awake in my dreams
I'll call out to you in the dark
                              to discover the murmur of your breath
I'll call out to you in the dark
                              because you're awake in my dreams


clinging to the fire of your body
                              your dense paths
                                    your memories & desires
I want to be the tree of night
                              clinging to the fire of your body
I want to be the tree of night
                              your dense paths
                                    your memories & desires

# ABOUT YOU IF ANYONE'S ASKING

you confuse left & right
>>>> your smile makes me feel a superhero
you're amazing
>> you're stupid
>>>> you confuse left & right
you're amazing
>> you're stupid
>>> your smile makes me feel a superhero


you're an op from Dashiell Hammett
>>>> you're one of the Little Women
you're an earthquake
>>> an ocean
>>> you're an op from Dashiell Hammett
you're an earthquake
>>> an ocean
>>>> you're one of the Little Women


but the words
>> won't come out right
>>> as I stupidly try & talk to you
I'm in love
> & hungry
>>> & drunk
>>> but the words
>>>> won't come out right
I'm in love
>> & hungry
>>> & drunk
>>>> as I stupidly try & talk to you

# I NOTICE EVERY LITTLE THING ABOUT YOU

the unplanned gestures
                    the painted nails
                              the taste of skin
the touching & the stroking
                    the unplanned gestures
the touching & the stroking
                    the painted nails
                              the taste of skin


the shopping centre
          & café
                    & garden
                              this room covered with sounds
your scent is everywhere
                    the shopping centre
                              & café
                                   & garden
your scent is everywhere
                    this room covered with sounds


the way your breath is soft
                    how your eyes are stars & desire
& I thought
          I was in a dream
                    the way your breath is soft
& I thought
          I was in a dream
                    how your eyes are stars & desire

# WAKING TO LIFE

I call you & you bring
        the most expensive silks
                & the incantation of things
I look out of the window
           I call you & you bring
I look out of the window
          the most expensive silks
              & the incantation of things


you even walk over water
          your head is the sun
              & feet are the moon
the taste of paradise in my dreams
            you even walk over water
the taste of paradise in my dreams
           your head is the sun
              & feet are the moon


the perfume of machines & leaves
            I rub the sleep from my eyes
even the rain is very quiet
         the perfume of machines & leaves
even the rain is very quiet
         I rub the sleep from my eyes

# BABY HERE I COME

by Aberdonian
   convoy
     taxi
       jet-pack
        by Bon Accord

           kayak
by Comet
  beach buggy
     horse-back
      by Aberdonian
       convoy
        taxi
          jet-pack
by Comet
  beach buggy
     horse-back
      by Bon Accord
       kayak


by Golden Hind
   to your home
    & that's me carrying wine
      & a posy of lilacs
by Heart of Midlothian
    by Inter-City
      by Golden Hind
       to your home
by Heart of Midlothian
   by Inter-City
    & that's me carrying wine
      & a posy of lilacs

# COME DANCING

my rumba a rhapsody
        my quickstep a quatrain
                my cha-cha-cha an Italian Canzone
my salsa a sonnet that can't be faulted
        my rumba a rhapsody
                my quickstep a quatrain
my salsa a sonnet that can't be faulted
        my cha-cha-cha an Italian Canzone


my Charleston rich & stately
        as a chant royal
                my show dance a dazzling sestina
my fox trot numinous as free verse
                my Charleston rich & stately
                  as a chant royal
my fox trot numinous as free verse
        my show dance a dazzling sestina


I possess a slick fuselage made for dancing
        an antidote to this drear & stumbling life
the press write about my incestuous world
        I possess a slick fuselage made for dancing
the press write about my incestuous world
        an antidote to this drear & stumbling life

# THE SHEET OF NIGHT

the casual voice of night rolls through
                              like a breath or a kiss
all of a sudden darkness surrounds me
                    the casual voice of night rolls through
all of a sudden darkness surrounds me
                              like a breath or a kiss


on my knees
          praying to my love
                         exhaustion
                         tears through my body
I can't sleep on such a night
                    on my knees
                              praying to my love
I can't sleep on such a night
                    exhaustion
                         tears through my body


& my pleas are children's cries
                         but there's desire on my tongue
my love will always stay with me
                         & my pleas are children's cries
my love will always stay with me
                         but there's desire on my tongue

# TRAFFIC OF THE PAST

gripping the surface of a motorway
    speeding towards you the soft light of dawn
my heart is the wheel of a car
     gripping the surface of a motorway
my heart is the wheel of a car
    speeding towards you the soft light of dawn


of suburban streets glowing with your smile
       of hours with you
my heart holds the memory
    of suburban streets glowing with your smile
my heart holds the memory
    of hours with you


a roundabout
   a name of love
     only for you
      waiting
       engine purring
my heart is a sign
   a signal
    a roundabout
      a name of love
my heart is a sign
   a signal
   only for you
     waiting
      engine purring

## "OH HOW HAPPY"

about the 66 shades of Blue
                    of the deep Ocean Blue of your eyes
I have an Electric Blue desire to write
                    about the 66 Shades of Blue
I have an Electric Blue desire to write
                    of the deep Ocean Blue of your eyes


the bright Azure Blue of the sea
                    & the Cobalt Blue light falling like leaves
the Egyptian Blue of the afternoon
                    the bright Azure Blue of the sea
the Egyptian Blue of the afternoon
                    & the Cobalt Blue light falling like leaves


the Cornflower Blue of your kisses
                    & the Bondi Blue round your eyes
the Royal Blue warmth of your caresses
                    the Cornflower Blue of your kisses
the Royal Blue warmth of your caresses
                    & the Bondi Blue round your eyes

# HOW FAR WE MUST GO

to come from the planets
                              to leave behind a footprint of light
so many words are waiting for the poem
                              to come from the planets
so many words are waiting for the poem
                              to leave behind a footprint of light


from the sky down to the wildness
                              from blindness to brightness
your name has fallen from my lips
                              from the sky down to the wildness
your name has fallen from my lips
                              from blindness to brightness


in the sheer bliss of this verse
                              to end in an astonishment
                                              of a kiss
how simple it all is really
                              in the sheer bliss of this verse
how simple it all is really
                              to end in an astonishment
                                              of a kiss

# TOWARDS BRIGHT MOMENTS

or what being alive means
       or what happiness means
I'm 15 but I don't know what that means
       or what being alive means
I'm 15 but I don't know what that means
       or what happiness means


you were bruised behind the upright piano
       you were a flare
        a beacon
the band on stage were Heaven
     you were bruised behind the upright piano
the band on stage were Heaven
       you were a flare
        a beacon


I can't believe you've chosen me
    who wants to leap into the blue of your eyes
an innocent skinny schoolboy
       I can't believe you've chosen me
an innocent skinny schoolboy
    who wants to leap into the blue of your eyes

# WANDERING STILL IN PARADISE

I said *I do* after each sentence
                still have confetti in my jacket pocket
in the year of sun & strikes the death of Picasso
                    I said *I do* after each sentence
in the year of sun & strikes the death of Picasso
                still have confetti in my jacket pocket


& I've not lost my amour
                & you've not lost your allure
years later our mouths slower
                & I've not lost my amour
years later our mouths slower
                & you've not lost your allure


still our love's fuelled with rapture & spice
                I worship you a hundred times each day
the volume's right turned down
                still our love's fuelled with rapture & spice
the volume's right turned down
                I worship you a hundred times each day

# THERE ARE BIRDS HERE

the sweet notes of the nightingale
                                    if you come & sit beside me
and I will sing to you
                        the sweet notes of the nightingale
and I will sing to you
                        if you come & sit beside me


to be with you here
                through rain
                                hail & all that blows
long miles I've travelled
                        to be with you here
long miles I've travelled
                        through rain
                                hail & all that blows


give me your hand
                like lovers
                        we'll never be parted
come listen I will sing to you
                        give me your hand
come listen I will sing to you
                        like lovers
                                we'll never be parted

# IN THESE PAGES ARE BURNED OUT HOLES

when you are in love
         you want to write of desire & beauty & the heart
but it's impossible
         when you are in love
but it's impossible
         you want to write of desire & beauty & the heart


& show me the secret gate
         lead me to another world & its truth
take my hands
         & show me the secret gate
take my hands
         lead me to another world & its truth


when you are in love
         with everything that you are
         you want to write of desire & beauty
         but fail
but it's impossible
         when you are in love
         with everything that you are
but it's impossible
         you want to write of desire & beauty
         but fail

Printed in Great Britain
by Amazon

83846017R00029